DRIVING FOR DOLLARS

A Ride-Share Driver's Untold Story

The Realty Titan's Guide to Wholesaling Real Estate
without Using Your Own Money

Chris Buttrum

Table of Contents

About the Author, Chris Buttrum – The Realty Titan

Chris Buttrum is a highly experienced real estate professional with over 19 years of expertise in the industry. From his humble beginnings in 2001, when he embarked on his first rehab project, Chris has significantly impacted the real estate and investing world. As the co-owner of HomeWire Realty, a leading real estate agency, and the founder of NuGen Homes, a new home construction company, Chris is dedicated to transforming the real estate experience for buyers and sellers alike.

Chris' journey in real estate began as a young agent, working alongside banks to facilitate foreclosures and short sales. He gained invaluable experience listing properties and negotiating for his clients through his role. However, it was happening when he witnessed the darker side of the industry: agents hoarding inventory for personal gain, buyers struggling to determine fair property prices, and sellers grappling with understanding their home's value.

Motivated to bring about positive change, Chris recognized the need for transparency and fairness in real estate transactions. With the founding of HomeWire.com, an innovative platform allowing buyers and sellers to view real-time bids in one centralized location, Chris and his team revolutionized how properties are bought and sold. This auction dynamic brings transparency to the process, empowering buyers to bid confidently and enabling sellers to make informed pricing decisions. The result is faster sales, fairer prices, and a more efficient transaction process for all parties involved.

In addition to his contributions to HomeWire.com, Chris' venture into new home construction with NuGen Homes further expands his ability to provide buyers with quality, affordable housing options. By working with modular homes, manufactured homes, and panelized homes, Chris offers innovative solutions to meet the evolving needs of homebuyers.

With a solid commitment to customer service, Chris attributes his success to his background in retail, where he learned the importance of understanding clients and delivering world-class customer experiences. Chris brings this dedication to every interaction through his various ventures and companies, ensuring clients receive the highest service and support.

As a visionary leader in the real estate industry, Chris takes pride in the exceptional teams he has assembled and the cutting-edge platforms they have developed. Through HomeWire.com and NuGen Homes, he strives to provide a brighter future for buyers and sellers, empowering them to make better-informed decisions and investments.

With a wealth of experience, a passion for innovation, and an unwavering commitment to transparency and fairness, Chris Buttrum, known as The Realty Titan, continues to impact the real estate industry significantly.

Chapter 1: Introduction

- Why this book?
- Who should read this book?
- Setting realistic expectations

Chapter 2: The Power of Driving for Dollars

- Discovering the potential of real estate wholesaling
- Advantages for ride-share drivers
- Maximizing opportunities while driving

Chapter 3: Understanding Wholesaling and Distressed Properties

- Defining wholesaling in real estate
- Identifying distressed properties for wholesaling
- Recognizing profitable wholesale opportunities

Chapter 4: Transitioning from Poor to Wealthy

- Assessing your current financial situation
- Setting goals and aspirations
- Adopting a wealth-building mindset

Chapter 5: Building Your Real Estate Strategy

- Defining your wholesaling goals
- Researching local real estate markets
- Crafting a step-by-step plan for success

Chapter 6: Mastering the Art of Driving for Dollars

- Optimizing your ride-share time for wholesaling
- Systemizing your driving-for-dollars strategy
- Utilizing technology and tools for efficiency

Chapter 7: Identifying Distressed Properties

- Spotting distressed properties while driving

- Researching target neighborhoods for wholesale potential
- Developing relationships with distressed property owners

Chapter 8: Evaluating Investment Potential

- Conducting preliminary property assessments
- Estimating after-repair value (ARV) and repair costs
- Determining potential wholesale profits

Chapter 9: Wholesaling: The No-Money Down Approach

- Understanding the concept of no-money-down wholesaling
- Finding motivated sellers and cash buyers
- Analyzing profitable wholesale deals without personal funds

Chapter 10: Navigating the Wholesaling Process

- Building a solid wholesale team
- Creating contracts and agreements
- Managing legal and regulatory requirements

Chapter 11: Building a Network of Buyers and Sellers

- Cultivating relationships with cash buyers

- Developing a pipeline of motivated sellers
- Leveraging networking events and online platforms

Chapter 12: Negotiating Profitable Deals

- Techniques for successful negotiation in wholesaling
- Overcoming common objections from sellers and buyers
- Maximizing profit margins in wholesale transactions

Chapter 13: Closing Wholesaling Transactions

- Streamlining the closing process in wholesaling
- Managing documentation and paperwork
- Ensuring a smooth and successful transaction

Chapter 14: Scaling Up Your Wholesaling Business

- Expanding your wholesaling operations
- Managing multiple deals simultaneously
- Leveraging automation and delegation

Chapter 15: Leveraging Your Ride-Share Income

- Maximizing your ride-share earnings for real estate investments
- Allocating funds for wholesaling ventures

- Balancing time commitments between driving and wholesaling

Chapter 16: Overcoming Challenges and Risks

- Dealing with obstacles and setbacks in wholesaling
- Mitigating financial and legal risks
- Developing resilience and persistence

Chapter 17: The Power of Marketing and Branding

- Creating a solid brand as a wholesaling ride-share driver
- Implementing effective marketing strategies
- Leveraging online platforms and social media

Chapter 18: The Future of Wholesaling as a Ride-Share Driver

- Embracing technological advancements in wholesaling
- Predictions for the real estate industry
- Continuing education and growth opportunities

Conclusion

- Recap of key strategies and concepts
- Encouragement for readers to take action

Appendix

- Recommended resources for further learning
- Glossary of real estate and wholesaling terms
- Worksheets and templates for analysis

Disclaimer: The information provided in this book is for educational purposes only. It is not intended as financial or legal advice. Readers should consult with professionals before making any investment or business decisions.

Introduction

Welcome to "Driving for Dollars: A Ride-Share Driver's Untold Story - The Realty Titan's Guide to Wholesaling Real Estate without Using Your Own Money." In this introduction, we embark on a journey to redefine your perception of wealth creation and empower you to take control of your financial destiny.

Are you a ride-share driver who dreams of breaking free from the chains of financial struggle? Are you seeking a path to wealth and success that leverages your unique position behind the wheel? Look no further. This book is crafted explicitly for ambitious ride-share drivers like you who aspire to turn their driving time into a gateway to real estate riches.

In these pages, you will uncover the hidden potential within the intersections of driving people around town and unearthing distressed properties. This untold story reveals the remarkable world of wholesaling, which allows you to profit from distressed properties without needing personal funds.

Imagine the power of driving through your city streets, ferrying passengers from one destination to another, all while honing your observation skills and spotting the telltale signs of distressed properties. Overgrown grass, neglected homes, and piled-up mail become your treasure map, guiding you to profitable opportunities that others may overlook.

Wholesaling is at the heart of this journey. It involves finding motivated sellers, securing contracts for distressed properties, and assigning them to cash buyers for a fee. The beauty of wholesaling lies in its accessibility, as it requires little to no upfront capital. By mastering the art of wholesaling, you can go from a ride-share driver struggling to make ends meet to a real estate entrepreneur building a pathway to lasting wealth.

This book teaches you the ins and outs of "Driving for Dollars" as a ride-share driver. You will discover how to identify distressed properties, evaluate their investment potential, negotiate profitable deals, and close successful wholesale transactions. Additionally, you will gain insights into scaling up your wholesaling business, leveraging your ride-share income, overcoming challenges and risks, and building a solid brand and network.

However, let us be clear: success requires effort, dedication, and a willingness to learn. This book is not a promise of overnight riches but a roadmap to guide your journey. You must take action, apply the principles and strategies outlined, and adapt them to your unique circumstances.

Are you ready to transform your ride-share hustle into a thriving real estate business? Are you prepared to embrace the opportunities that "Driving for Dollars" presents? If so, buckle up, for your untold story is about to unfold.

Join me on this remarkable adventure as we uncover the secrets of wholesaling real estate as a ride-share driver. Together, we will break through financial barriers and unlock a world of possibilities. It's time to rewrite your future and become the Realty Titan you were destined to be.

Why this book? This book aims to empower ride-share drivers like you to leverage your unique position and discover the untapped potential of real estate wholesaling. Combining your ride-share job with strategically pursuing distressed properties can unlock a path to financial abundance and transform your life.

Who should read this book? This book is designed explicitly for ride-share drivers who aspire to break free from the constraints of financial hardship and explore the possibilities that real estate wholesaling offers. Whether you're a new driver or have been in the ride-share industry for a while, this guide will provide the knowledge and tools to embark on your wholesaling journey.

Setting realistic expectations: While the opportunities presented in this book are promising, it is essential to set realistic expectations. Building wealth through real estate wholesaling requires dedication, persistence, and a willingness to learn. This book will provide guidance, but success ultimately depends on your drive and commitment to action.

Throughout this journey, we will explore the art of "Driving for Dollars," a unique strategy that allows you to identify distressed properties while working as a ride-share driver. By recognizing the signs of neglect, such as overgrown grass, weeds, and piled-up mail, you will uncover hidden opportunities for profitable real estate wholesaling.

The concept of wholesaling will be at the heart of this book. Wholesaling involves finding motivated sellers, securing contracts for distressed properties, and assigning those contracts to cash buyers for a fee. The best part? You can achieve this without using your money, making wholesaling an accessible avenue for wealth creation.

Are you ready to embark on this incredible journey? Join me as we delve into the world of "Driving for Dollars" and learn how to leverage your ride-share income to become a successful real estate wholesaler. Let's turn your dreams of financial freedom into a reality!

Unveiling the Ride-Share Driver's Potential

This chapter will dive into the untapped potential within the ride-share driver's unique position and explore the transformative power of combining ride-sharing with real estate wholesaling.

1.1 The Ride-Share Advantage:

As a ride-share driver, you possess a valuable advantage that differentiates you from traditional real estate investors. Your time behind the wheel provides a unique opportunity to observe your city's neighborhoods, discover hidden pockets of distress, and uncover potential real estate deals others may overlook. While driving passengers from point A to point B, you have a front-row seat to the ever-changing landscape of properties, both well-maintained and neglected.

1.2 Recognizing Distressed Properties:

In this section, we will explore the signs and characteristics of distressed properties. You can uncover hidden gems with significant profit potential by developing an eye for identifying distressed homes. We will delve into the visual cues of neglect, such as overgrown lawns, boarded-up windows, dilapidated exteriors, and other telltale signs that indicate a property is distressed.

1.3 The Wholesaling Opportunity:

Wholesaling is a powerful real estate strategy that allows you to capitalize on distressed properties without the need for substantial capital or credit. As a ride-share driver, you are uniquely positioned to take advantage of this strategy. Wholesaling involves finding motivated sellers, negotiating contracts, and assigning those contracts to cash buyers for a fee, effectively acting as the intermediary in the transaction.

1.4 Building the Foundation:

To embark on your journey as a real estate wholesaler, it is crucial to lay a solid foundation. This section will guide you through assessing your current financial situation, setting realistic goals, and adopting a wealth-building mindset. We will explore the importance of mindset shifts and the determination required to succeed in the real estate industry.

1.5 Crafting Your Wholesaling Strategy:

Every successful venture requires a well-thought-out strategy. This section will discuss the critical components of building your real estate wholesaling strategy. You will learn to define your target market, research local real estate trends, and create a step-by-step plan to guide your journey. A strategic approach will help you navigate the challenges and maximize the opportunities that lie ahead.

1.6 Embracing the Journey:

As we conclude Chapter 1, I invite you to embrace the journey before you. The world of real estate wholesaling offers a remarkable opportunity for rideshare drivers to go from financial struggle to wealth creation. By leveraging your unique position, combining ride-sharing with driving for dollars, and engaging in wholesaling, you have the potential to transform your life and create a future filled with financial abundance.

In the upcoming chapters, we will dive deeper into the art of driving for dollars, identifying distressed properties, evaluating their investment potential, and mastering the wholesaling process. Get ready to unlock your full potential as a ride-share driver turned real estate entrepreneur.

Chapter 2

The Power of Driving for Dollars

This chapter will explore the incredible power of driving for dollars and how it can become your key to unlocking profitable real estate opportunities.

2.1 The Wholesaling Advantage:

You possess a unique advantage in wholesaling real estate as a ride-share driver. Daily journeys through city streets provide an unmatched opportunity to discover distressed properties others may overlook. Combining your ride-share job with pursuing distressed properties can transform your driving time into a treasure hunt for lucrative real estate deals.

2.2 Maximizing Your Ride-Share Time:

This section will discuss strategies to maximize your ride-share time for driving for dollars. You will learn how to optimize your routes, allocate specific periods for scouting potential deals, and leverage technology to streamline your efforts. Making minor adjustments to your routine can significantly increase your chances of finding valuable distressed properties.

2.3 The Art of Observation:

Developing a keen eye for identifying distressed properties is a skill that will set you apart as a successful ride-share driver turned real estate wholesaler. We will explore the visual cues of neglect, such as overgrown lawns, boarded-up windows, noticeable deterioration, and other indicators that a property may be distressed. By honing your powers of observation, you will spot opportunities that others may pass by.

2.4 Researching Target Neighborhoods:

To make the most of your driving-for-dollars strategy, it is crucial to research and focus on target neighborhoods that hold potential for distressed properties. We will discuss methods for identifying neighborhoods with a higher likelihood of housing distressed properties, such as areas experiencing economic shifts, high foreclosure rates, or visible signs of neglect. This knowledge will empower you to direct your efforts where they are most likely to yield fruitful results.

2.5 Building Relationships with Locals:

Networking and building relationships with locals are essential components of driving-for-dollars success. In this section, we will explore strategies for connecting with individuals who have their finger on the pulse of the local real estate market. From real estate agents and property managers to neighborhood associations and community members, these connections can provide valuable insights, leads, and potential partnerships.

2.6 The Mindset of a Driving-for-Dollars Wholesaler:

As we conclude Chapter 2, we will discuss the importance of adopting the mindset of a driving-for-dollars wholesaler. We will delve into the mindset shifts required to succeed in real estate wholesaling, including persistence, resilience, and a commitment to ongoing learning and growth. By cultivating a mindset of opportunity and abundance, you will approach your driving-for-dollars journey with confidence and determination.

Get ready to harness the power of driving for dollars and uncover hidden treasures with every mile you drive. In the upcoming chapters, we will further explore identifying distressed properties, evaluating their investment potential, and mastering wholesaling. Your journey towards financial free-dom and wealth creation as a ride-share driver turned real estate wholesaler is well underway.

Chapter 3

Understanding Wholesaling and Distressed Properties

In this chapter, we will delve into the fundamental concepts of wholesaling and the importance of understanding distressed properties in your journey toward real estate wealth.

3.1 Wholesaling: An Overview:

Wholesaling is a powerful strategy that allows you to profit from real estate transactions without the need for substantial capital or credit. In this section, we will provide an in-depth overview of wholesaling, explaining its fundamental principles, processes, and the role you, as a ride-share driver, can play in this lucrative venture. Understanding the fundamentals of wholesaling is essential for building a solid foundation as a successful real estate wholesaler.

3.2 The Distressed Property Market:

Distressed properties form the cornerstone of wholesaling real estate. In this section, we will explore the concept of distressed properties, including their characteristics and why they present unique opportunities for real estate investors. From properties facing foreclosure to neglected homes needing repair, understanding the distressed property market is crucial for identifying potential deals and maximizing your wholesaling profits.

3.3 Identifying Distressed Properties:

Recognizing distressed properties is a skill that will set you apart as a successful wholesaler. This section will delve deeper into the visual cues and indicators of distressed properties you should know while driving for dollars. From overgrown yards and boarded-up windows to signs of neglect and deferred maintenance, honing your ability to spot distressed properties will give you a competitive edge in the market.

3.4 Evaluating Investment Potential:

Once you've identified distressed properties, the next step is to evaluate their investment potential. In this section, we will discuss the factors to consider when assessing the profitability of a potential wholesale deal. You will learn how to estimate the after-repair value (ARV), evaluate repair costs, and calculate potential wholesale profits. Developing these analytical skills will enable you to make informed decisions and focus your efforts on the most lucrative opportunities.

3.5 The Motivated Seller:

Motivated sellers play a vital role in the wholesaling process. In this section, we will explore the concept of motivated sellers and discuss why they are crucial for successful wholesale deals. Understanding the motivations behind a seller's desire to sell their distressed property quickly will empower you to approach negotiations with empathy, professionalism, and the ability to secure favorable deals.

3.6 Building a Wholesaling Network:

Building a solid network is instrumental in the world of wholesaling. In this section, we will discuss the importance of cultivating relationships with cash buyers, fellow investors, real estate agents, and other key players in the industry. Networking allows you to expand your buyer's list, gain access to off-market deals, and collaborate with like-minded professionals. We will provide insights on effective networking strategies and platforms to help you establish and grow your wholesaling network.

As we conclude Chapter 3, you have a solid foundation for wholesaling and understanding distressed properties. In the upcoming chapters, we will explore the strategies and techniques to navigate the wholesaling process, negotiate profitable deals, and close successful transactions. Get ready to take your wholesaling journey to the next level as we continue the path to real estate wealth.

Chapter 4

Transitioning from Poor to Wealthy

In this chapter, we will explore the crucial steps needed to transition from a state of financial struggle to a path of wealth creation through real estate wholesaling.

4.1 Assessing Your Current Financial Situation:

Assessing your current financial situation is essential to embark on the journey toward wealth creation. In this section, we will guide you through a self-assessment process, helping you gain clarity on your income, expenses, debts, and savings. Understanding your financial position will serve as a starting point for setting realistic goals and developing a plan for your wealth-building journey.

4.2 Setting Goals and Aspirations:

Setting clear goals is vital for driving your financial transformation. This section will discuss the importance of setting specific, measurable, achievable, relevant, and time-bound (SMART) goals. Whether paying off debts, saving for investments, or achieving a certain income level, setting goals will provide direction and motivation as you navigate the world of real estate wholesaling.

4.3 Adopting a Wealth-Building Mindset:

A wealth-building mindset is essential for transforming your financial reality. This section will explore the mindset shifts necessary to cultivate an abundance mentality, overcome limiting beliefs, and embrace a positive outlook on wealth creation. By adopting a mindset focused on growth, resilience, and continuous learning, you will develop the mental fortitude needed to overcome obstacles and achieve success.

4.4 Embracing Education and Knowledge:

Education and knowledge are the cornerstones of your journey from financial struggle to wealth creation. This section will discuss the importance of ongoing education and the various resources available to expand your knowledge in real estate wholesaling. From books and online courses to seminars and networking events, we will explore avenues for acquiring the necessary skills and expertise to thrive in the industry.

4.5 Taking Action:

Taking consistent and focused action is the key to turning your aspirations into reality. This section will discuss the importance of developing a disciplined work ethic, setting priorities, and implementing effective time management strategies. We will also explore the concept of "fail forward," emphasizing the value of learning from setbacks and using them as stepping stones to success.

4.6 Seeking Support and Accountability:

Building a support system and finding accountability partners are critical elements of your journey. This section will explore the benefits of surrounding yourself with like-minded individuals who share your vision for success. We will discuss the importance of seeking mentors, joining real estate investor groups, and engaging in mastermind sessions to gain support, guidance, and motivation.

As we conclude Chapter 4, you now have a solid understanding of the initial steps needed to transition from a state of financial struggle to a path of wealth creation through real estate wholesaling. In the upcoming chapters, we will delve deeper into the specific strategies and techniques required to excel in wholesaling, negotiate profitable deals, and build a thriving real estate business. Get ready to transform your financial reality as you continue your journey toward real estate wealth.

Chapter 5

Building Your Real Estate Strategy

In this chapter, we will focus on building a robust real estate strategy that will guide you toward success in the world of wholesaling.

5.1 Defining Your Wholesaling Goals:

Defining your wholesaling goals is essential to build an effective real estate strategy. This section will explore the different aspects of goal setting, including short-term and long-term objectives, financial targets, and personal aspirations. By clarifying your goals, you will have a clear roadmap to follow and a sense of purpose as you navigate the world of wholesaling.

5.2 Researching Local Real Estate Markets:

Understanding the local real estate market is crucial for developing a successful strategy. This section will discuss the importance of researching and analyzing your target market. You will learn how to assess market trends, identify areas with high potential for distressed properties, and gather data on property values, rental rates, and market demand. This knowledge will enable you to make informed decisions and focus your efforts where they are most likely to yield fruitful results.

5.3 Crafting a Step-by-Step Plan:

A well-crafted plan is essential for achieving your wholesaling goals. This section will guide you through developing a step-by-step plan that aligns with your goals and market research. We will explore the critical components of a wholesaling plan, including lead-generation strategies, marketing tactics, networking efforts, deal analysis, and the overall timeline for your wholesaling business. By outlining your plan, you will have a roadmap and a clear understanding of the actions required to succeed.

5.4 Allocating Resources:

Effective resource allocation is vital for executing your real estate strategy. This section will discuss allocating resources such as time, finances, and energy. You will learn how to optimize your ride-share income, set aside marketing and lead generation funds, and manage your time efficiently to balance your driving responsibilities with wholesaling activities. By strategically allocating your resources, you will maximize your chances of success in wholesaling.

5.5 Leveraging Technology and Tools:

In today's digital age, leveraging technology and tools can significantly enhance your wholesaling efforts. This section will explore the technological resources available to streamline your wholesaling business. We will discuss customer relationship management (CRM) systems, online lead generation, marketing platforms, financial analysis tools, and communication platforms for networking and collaboration. By utilizing these tools effectively, you can gain a competitive edge and increase your efficiency as a wholesaler.

5.6 Monitoring and Adjusting Your Strategy:

Building a successful real estate strategy requires continuous monitoring and adjustment. In this section, we will discuss the importance of tracking key performance indicators (KPIs) and analyzing the results of your wholesaling efforts. We will explore methods for evaluating the effectiveness of your strategies, identifying areas for improvement, and making necessary adjustments to optimize your success. Regularly monitoring and adjusting your strategy, you will stay ahead of the curve and adapt to changing market conditions.

As we conclude Chapter 5, you have a solid foundation for building your real estate strategy. In the upcoming chapters, we will delve deeper into the techniques and practices required to excel in wholesaling, from identifying distressed properties to negotiating profitable deals and closing successful transactions. Get ready to implement your strategy and take your wholesaling journey to the next level.

Chapter 6:

Mastering the Art of Driving for Dollars

In this chapter, we will dive deep into the art of driving for dollars and explore how you can optimize your ride-share time for maximum success in identifying distressed properties.

6.1 The Importance of Efficiency:

Efficiency is vital when it comes to driving for dollars. This section will discuss the significance of optimizing your driving routes, managing your time effectively, and minimizing distractions on the road. Maximizing your efficiency can cover more ground, increase the number of properties you encounter, and improve your chances of finding lucrative distressed property opportunities.

6.2 Systemizing Your Driving-for-Dollars Strategy:

To achieve consistent results, it is crucial to systemize your driving-for-dollars strategy. In this section, we will explore the process of developing a systematic approach to your property scouting efforts. We will discuss the importance of documenting and organizing your findings, leveraging technology to streamline your data collection, and establishing a routine that allows you to track and follow up on potential deals efficiently.

6.3 Utilizing Technology and Tools:

Technology can be a game-changer when it comes to driving for dollars. This section will explore the technology and tools available to enhance your property scouting efforts. From smartphone apps that help you track property details to mapping tools that optimize your driving routes, we will explore how leveraging technology can save you time, increase productivity, and improve your overall success rate.

6.4 Leveraging Data and Analytics:

Data and analytics can provide valuable insights that inform your driving-for-dollars strategy. This section will discuss the importance of analyzing and interpreting the data you collect during your property scouting expeditions. We will explore how data points such as property characteristics, market trends, and historical sales information can guide your decision-making process and help you identify the most promising distressed properties for potential wholesale deals.

6.5 Developing Observation Skills:

Observing and identifying distressed properties is a skill that can be honed over time. This section will delve deeper into developing your observation skills while driving for dollars. We will explore techniques for noticing subtle signs of distress, such as neglected exteriors, necessary repairs, and other indicators that a property may be a potential wholesale opportunity. You will become more adept at identifying distressed properties in your target areas by sharpening your observation skills.

6.6 Balancing Ride-Share and Property Scouting:

Finding the right balance between your ride-share responsibilities and property scouting efforts is essential. This section will discuss strategies for effectively managing your time and energy to accommodate both aspects of your journey. We will explore techniques for incorporating property scouting into your ride-share routine, setting designated property scouting periods, and maintaining a flexible schedule that allows you to capitalize on potential opportunities.

As we conclude Chapter 6, you understand the art of driving for dollars. In the upcoming chapters, we will further explore the techniques and practices required to identify distressed properties, evaluate their investment potential, negotiate profitable deals, and close successful transactions. Get ready to elevate your driving-for-dollars game and accelerate your progress as a real estate wholesaler.

Chapter 7

Identifying Distressed Properties: Needles in a Haystack

In this chapter, we will dive into the art of identifying distressed properties—the hidden gems with the potential for profitable wholesale deals. Get ready to uncover those needles in a haystack and transform them into opportunities for financial success.

7.1 Understanding Distressed Property Categories:

Distressed properties come in various forms, each presenting unique opportunities. In this section, we will explore the different categories of distressed properties, including:

1. Pre-foreclosures: Properties where the owners have fallen behind on mortgage payments and may be at risk of foreclosure.

2.   Foreclosures: Properties seized by lenders due to non-payment of mortgages.

3.   REOs (Real Estate Owned): Properties that have been repossessed by lenders and are now bank-owned.

4.   Vacant Properties: Properties that are unoccupied and show signs of neglect or abandonment.

5.   Probate Properties: Properties that are part of an estate being settled through probate, often with motivated sellers.

6.   Distressed Sellers: Homeowners facing financial or personal hardships, such as divorce, job loss, or necessary repairs.

Understanding the different categories of distressed properties will enable you to target your efforts and focus on the areas with the highest potential for profitable wholesale deals.

7.2 Spotting Distressed Property Indicators:

Spotting the indicators of distressed properties is an art that requires a keen eye and attention to detail. This section will explore the common indicators that a property may be distressed. These indicators may include:

1. Overgrown or neglected landscaping

2. Boarded-up windows or doors

3. Visible signs of damage or disrepair

4. Accumulated trash or debris

5. Absence of utilities or disconnected services

6. Notices of foreclosure or auction posted on the property

You can quickly identify potential wholesale opportunities by developing your ability to spot these indicators while driving for dollars.

7.3 Gathering Property Information:

Once you've identified a potentially distressed property, gathering critical information is essential for further evaluation. In this section, we will discuss strategies for gathering property information. This may involve taking notes, capturing photographs, documenting the property's address and contact information, and conducting additional research on public records and online resources. The more information you collect, the better equipped you will be to evaluate the property's investment potential.

7.4 Assessing Investment Potential:

Evaluating the investment potential of a distressed property is a critical step in the wholesaling process. This section will explore the factors to consider when assessing investment potential. This includes evaluating the property's location, condition, repair costs, market value, and comparable sales. We will discuss techniques for conducting a thorough analysis and determining whether the property has the potential for a profitable wholesale deal.

7.5 Engaging with Property Owners:

Engaging with property owners is essential to driving for dollars and wholesaling. This section will explore strategies for approaching property owners, initiating conversations, and building rapport. We will discuss the importance of empathy, understanding the seller's motivation, and tailoring your approach to each situation. Building trust and establishing positive relationships with property owners can significantly increase your chances of securing wholesale deals.

7.6 Documenting and Organizing Property Leads:

As you encounter multiple distressed properties, it becomes essential to document and organize your property leads effectively. This section will discuss methods for documenting property information, utilizing technology to streamline lead management, and establishing a system for organizing your leads. Proper documentation and organization will ensure you can track and follow up on potential deals efficiently.

As we conclude Chapter 7, you now have a deeper understanding of identifying distressed properties—a crucial skill in wholesaling. In the upcoming chapters, we will further explore the techniques and practices required to negotiate profitable deals, secure contracts, and close successful wholesale transactions. Get ready to turn those identified distressed properties into lucrative opportunities on your journey to real estate wealth.

Chapter 8:

Negotiating Profitable Deals

This chapter will explore the art of negotiating profitable deals—the crucial skill to turn your identified distressed properties into successful wholesale transactions. Get ready to master the negotiation process and maximize your profits in the world of wholesaling.

8.1 Understanding the Power of Negotiation:

Negotiation is a fundamental skill in the world of real estate wholesaling. In this section, we will discuss the importance of understanding the power of negotiation and its impact on your ability to secure favorable deals. We will explore the critical elements of successful negotiations, including effective communication, active listening, and the ability to find mutually beneficial solutions.

8.2 Preparing for Negotiations:

Preparation is vital to successful negotiations. This section will discuss the steps involved in preparing for negotiations. This includes conducting thorough research on the property, understanding the seller's motivation, establishing your desired outcome and walk-away point, and developing a negotiation strategy. By being well-prepared, you can confidently approach negotiations and increase your chances of achieving profitable outcomes.

8.3 Building Rapport with Sellers:

Building rapport with sellers is a crucial aspect of successful negotiations. This section will explore strategies for establishing connections and fostering trust with sellers. We will discuss the importance of active listening, empathy, and effective communication. Building rapport can create a positive atmosphere for negotiations and increase the likelihood of reaching mutually beneficial agreements.

8.4 Presenting Your Offer:

Presenting your offer effectively is essential in negotiations. This section will discuss the components of a persuasive offer presentation. We will explore techniques for highlighting the benefits of your offer, addressing the seller's concerns, and showcasing your credibility as a serious buyer. By compellingly presenting your offer, you can increase the seller's chances of accepting your terms.

8.5 Negotiating Win-Win Solutions:

Negotiating win-win solutions is the ultimate goal in wholesaling. In this section, we will explore strategies for finding mutually beneficial outcomes that satisfy both you as the wholesaler and the seller. We will discuss techniques for identifying the seller's underlying needs, exploring creative solutions, and compromising where necessary. By focusing on win-win solutions, you can establish long-lasting relationships and lay the foundation for future successful transactions.

8.6 Handling Challenges and Objections:

Challenges and objections are common in negotiations. This section will explore strategies for handling objections effectively and overcoming challenges that may arise during the negotiation process. We will discuss techniques for addressing common objections, reframing objections as opportunities, and maintaining a solution-oriented mindset. You can navigate through obstacles and reach successful agreements by proactively addressing challenges.

8.7 Securing Contracts and Closing Deals:

Securing contracts and closing deals is the final step in the negotiation process. This section will discuss the importance of effectively documenting agreements and meeting all necessary legal requirements. We will explore the process of drafting and presenting contracts, conducting due diligence, and working with legal professionals to finalize the transaction. You can confidently move towards closing the deal by ensuring a smooth contract process.

As we conclude Chapter 8, you now have a deeper understanding of negotiating profitable deals—an essential skill in wholesaling. In the upcoming chapters, we will further explore the techniques and practices required to close successful wholesale transactions, assign contracts, and ensure a smooth transition of properties to cash buyers. Get ready to elevate your negotiation skills and maximize your profits on your journey to real estate wealth.

Chapter 9:

Closing Successful Wholesale Transactions

Introduction:

In this chapter, we will focus on the crucial steps involved in closing successful wholesale transactions. From assigning contracts to ensuring a smooth transition of properties to cash buyers, this chapter will guide you through the final stages of the wholesaling process.

9.1 Reviewing and Finalizing Contracts:

Reviewing and finalizing contracts is a critical step in the closing process. This section will discuss the importance of carefully reviewing all contract terms, including purchase agreements, assignment contracts, and other relevant documents. We will explore strategies for ensuring the accuracy and completeness of contracts, seeking legal advice when necessary, and addressing any concerns or modifications before proceeding.

9.2 Coordinating with Buyers and Sellers:

Coordinating with both the buyer and the seller is essential for a smooth transaction. This section will discuss the importance of effective communication and coordination with all parties involved. We will explore strategies to keep all parties informed about the transaction's progress, address any concerns or questions, and facilitate a collaborative environment that ensures a seamless closing process.

9.3 Conducting Due Diligence:

Conducting due diligence is crucial to ensure the property's condition and legal status. This section will explore the steps involved in conducting thorough due diligence, such as property inspections, title searches, and reviewing existing liens or encumbrances. We will discuss the importance of mitigating risks and ensuring that the property suits the cash buyer.

9.4 Assigning Contracts:

Assigning contracts is a crucial aspect of the wholesale process. This section will delve into assigning your contract to the cash buyer. We will discuss the documentation and procedures for transferring the contract rights and obligations to the buyer. We will also explore strategies to ensure a smooth assignment process and maintain transparency and open communication with all parties involved.

9.5 Coordinating the Closing:

Coordinating the closing of the wholesale transaction is essential for a successful outcome. This section will discuss the coordination and logistics involved in the closing process, including scheduling the closing date, arranging for funds transfer, and overseeing the signing of documents. We will explore strategies for managing last-minute issues and ensuring the closing process is completed efficiently.

9.6 Ensuring a Smooth Transition:

Ensuring a smooth transition of the property to the cash buyer is the final step in closing a wholesale transaction. This section will discuss the importance of facilitating a seamless property handover. We will explore strategies for coordinating with all parties involved, overseeing any necessary repairs or cleanup, and ensuring that the property is delivered according to the contract's agreed-upon condition.

9.7 Celebrating Success and Reflecting:

As we conclude Chapter 9, take a moment to celebrate your success in closing a wholesale transaction. Reflect on your journey—from identifying distressed properties to negotiating profitable deals and closing successful transactions. Acknowledge your achievements and the valuable lessons learned along the way. By celebrating your successes and reflecting on your experiences, you can continue to refine your wholesaling skills and build a prosperous real estate business.

In the final chapter, we will wrap up our journey and guide you on maintaining success, scaling your wholesaling business, and growing as a real estate entrepreneur. Get ready to embark on the next phase of your journey and embrace the opportunities.

Chapter 10

Scaling Your Wholesaling Business

This chapter will explore strategies for scaling your wholesaling business and achieving new heights. As you reflect on your journey and celebrate your successes, it's time to plan for the future and expand your real estate empire.

10.1 Setting Ambitious Goals:

Setting ambitious goals is crucial for scaling your wholesaling business. This section will discuss the importance of setting challenging yet achievable goals. We will explore methods for defining your vision, breaking your goals into manageable milestones, and establishing a roadmap for growth. Setting ambitious goals can fuel your motivation and drive your business toward success.

10.2 Building a Team:

Building a competent and reliable team is essential for scaling your wholesaling business. This section will explore the roles and responsibilities needed to support and grow your operations. We will discuss strategies for recruiting and hiring team members, such as real estate agents, property inspectors, marketing professionals, and administrative staff. Building a strong team will allow you to leverage the expertise of others and focus on strategic business growth.

10.3 Streamlining Operations:

Streamlining your operations is critical to managing increased volume and maintaining efficiency. This section will discuss strategies for optimizing your processes, implementing automation and technology tools, and delegating tasks effectively. By streamlining your operations, you can handle more wholesale deals and ensure your business operates smoothly and efficiently.

10.4 Expanding Your Marketing Efforts:

Expanding your marketing efforts is crucial for reaching a wider audience and generating more leads. This section will explore strategies for expanding your marketing channels, such as online advertising, direct mail campaigns, networking events, and partnerships with local professionals. We will discuss the importance of branding, creating a strong online presence, and developing targeted marketing campaigns to attract motivated sellers and cash buyers.

10.5 Building Relationships with Cash Buyers:

Building solid relationships with cash buyers is vital for scaling your wholesaling business. This section will discuss strategies for expanding your network of cash buyers, including attending real estate investor meetups, joining investment groups, and leveraging online platforms. We will explore techniques for nurturing relationships with cash buyers and becoming their go-to wholesaler for profitable deals.

10.6 Continuing Education and Professional Development:

Continuing education and professional development are essential for staying ahead in the ever-evolving real estate industry. This section will discuss the importance of ongoing learning, workshops, seminars, and seeking mentorship from experienced real estate professionals. By continuously improving your knowledge and skills, you can adapt to market trends, expand your expertise, and remain a successful real estate wholesaler.

10.7 Giving Back to the Community:

As you scale your wholesaling business, giving back to the community that supports you is essential. In this section, we will explore the benefits of philanthropy and community involvement. We will discuss ways to contribute to charitable causes, support local organizations, and participate in initiatives that positively impact your community. Giving back benefits others enhances your reputation, and fosters goodwill.

10.8 Embracing Growth and Adaptation:

As you conclude your journey through this book, embrace growth and adaptation. The real estate industry is dynamic, and success comes to those willing to adapt to changing market conditions. Stay agile, open to new opportunities, and continuously seek ways to improve and innovate your business. By embracing growth and adaptation, you can stay ahead of the curve and build a thriving wholesaling business.

Chapter 11

The Journey Continues: Sustaining Success and Beyond

This chapter will explore strategies for sustaining your success as a real estate wholesaler and venturing into new opportunities. As you reflect on your achievements and look toward the future, it's time to continue your journey with passion and purpose.

11.1 Reviewing and Reflecting on Your Success:

Reviewing and reflecting on your success is essential to sustaining your achievements. This section will discuss the significance of reviewing your progress, analyzing your wins and challenges, and learning from your experiences. By taking time to reflect, you can gain valuable insights that will guide you on your ongoing journey of growth and improvement.

11.2 Cultivating a Growth Mindset:

Cultivating a growth mindset is crucial for continued success. This section will explore the power of a growth mindset - a belief that abilities and intelligence can be developed through dedication and hard work. We will discuss strategies for embracing challenges, seeking feedback, and maintaining a mindset focused on learning and improvement. You can overcome obstacles and continuously evolve as a real estate wholesaler by cultivating a growth mindset.

11.3 Expanding into New Real Estate Ventures:

As you solidify your position as a successful wholesaler, consider expanding into new real estate ventures. In this section, we will discuss the possibilities of diversifying your real estate portfolio through options such as fix and flip projects, buy and hold investments, or even exploring commercial real estate opportunities. We will explore the benefits, challenges, and strategies for venturing into new ventures and expanding your real estate empire.

11.4 Leveraging Technology and Innovation:

Technology and innovation can play a pivotal role in sustaining your success. This section will explore leveraging technology and embracing innovative tools and strategies in your wholesaling business. We will discuss emerging technologies, such as artificial intelligence, automation, and digital marketing techniques, that can enhance your operations, increase efficiency, and give you a competitive edge.

11.5 Nurturing Relationships and Building a Reputation:

Nurturing relationships and building a solid reputation are critical elements of sustaining success in the real estate industry. This section will discuss the importance of maintaining strong relationships with buyers, sellers, and industry professionals. We will explore strategies for providing exceptional customer service, fostering trust and transparency, and staying connected with your network. By nurturing relationships and building a solid reputation, you can generate repeat business and referrals, solidifying your position as a reputable wholesaler.

11.6 Giving Back to the Real Estate Community:

Giving back to the real estate community is an opportunity to contribute to the industry and leave a lasting impact. This section will discuss the benefits of sharing your knowledge and experiences with others through mentoring, speaking engagements, or contributing to real estate forums and publications. By giving back, you can inspire and empower aspiring wholesalers while continuing to learn and grow.

11.7 Maintaining Work-Life Balance:

Maintaining a healthy work-life balance is essential for long-term success and personal fulfillment. This section will explore strategies for managing time, setting boundaries, and prioritizing self-care. We will discuss the importance of finding harmony between your professional and personal life, ensuring that you have the energy and well-being to sustain your success in the long run.

11.8 Embracing the Journey:

As you conclude this book, embrace the ongoing journey of your real estate wholesaling career. Celebrate your successes, learn from your challenges, and push yourself towards new horizons. Remember that success is not a destination but an ever-evolving process. Embrace the opportunities, adapt to changes, and remain dedicated to your vision. The journey continues, and with each step, you have the potential to achieve even greater heights.

Congratulations on completing "Driving for Dollars: A Ride-Share Driver's Untold Story." You have equipped yourself with valuable knowledge, skills, and strategies to thrive in real estate wholesaling. As you move forward, stay committed to continuous growth, learning, and making a positive impact in the industry. Your journey as a successful real estate wholesaler is just beginning.

Your Wholesaling Success Roadmap

Introduction:

Welcome to Chapter 12, the bonus chapter of "Driving for Dollars: A Ride-Share Driver's Untold Story - The Realty Titan's Guide to Wholesaling Real Estate without Using Your Own Money." This final chapter will provide a comprehensive roadmap for your ongoing success as a real estate wholesaler. By following this roadmap, you will have a clear path to navigate, refine your strategies, and achieve your goals in the world of wholesaling.

12.1 Revisit Your Wholesaling Goals:

Start by revisiting your wholesaling goals and reflecting on your journey so far. This section will discuss the importance of regularly reassessing and updating your goals. Take the time to evaluate your progress, celebrate your achievements, and identify areas where you can further improve. You will stay focused and motivated on your path to success by aligning your actions with your goals.

12.2 Refine Your Strategies:

Successful wholesalers constantly refine their strategies to adapt to market conditions and evolving industry trends. In this section, we will explore the process of refining your strategies. Evaluate the effectiveness of your lead-generation methods, marketing campaigns, negotiation tactics, and overall operations. Identify areas for improvement and seek innovative approaches to enhance your efficiency and profitability.

12.3 Continuously Learn and Grow:

Continued learning and personal growth are essential for staying ahead in the real estate industry. This section will discuss strategies for ongoing education and professional development. Attend industry conferences, participate in workshops, join mastermind groups, and seek mentorship from experienced professionals. Embrace new technologies, trends, and best practices to remain at the forefront of the wholesaling field.

12.4 Leverage Technology and Automation:

Technology and automation can significantly streamline your wholesaling business and enhance your productivity. This section will explore the latest tools and software to automate tasks such as lead generation, marketing, customer relationship management, and deal tracking. Embrace digital platforms and technology solutions that can save you time, improve your organization, and allow you to focus on high-value activities.

12.5 Expand Your Network:

Building and expanding your professional network is vital for long-term success. This section will discuss the importance of networking and relationship-building in the real estate industry. Attend local real estate events, join industry associations, and connect with other professionals in the field. Nurture relationships with investors, real estate agents, contractors, and other key players who can support your wholesaling business and provide valuable insights and opportunities.

12.6 Stay Informed About Market Trends:

Staying informed about market trends and changes is crucial for making informed decisions and capitalizing on opportunities. This section will discuss strategies for staying updated on local market conditions, industry news, and regulatory changes. Follow real estate publications, subscribe to industry newsletters, and engage in online forums and discussion groups to stay connected with the latest developments.

12.7 Embrace a Mindset of Adaptability:

The real estate industry is dynamic and ever-changing. Embracing a mindset of adaptability is essential for long-term success. This section will discuss the importance of flexibility and openness to new ideas. Embrace change, be willing to pivot your strategies when necessary, and adapt to evolving market conditions. The ability to navigate uncertainties and seize new opportunities will set you apart as a successful wholesaler.

12.8 Seek Feedback and Testimonials:

Feedback and testimonials are powerful tools for building credibility and attracting new clients. This section will explore strategies for gathering feedback from sellers, cash buyers, and other stakeholders involved in your transactions. Request testimonials from satisfied clients and showcase them on your website, social media platforms, and marketing materials. Positive testimonials will strengthen your reputation and attract more business.

12.9 Give Back to the Wholesaling Community:

As you achieve success, remember to give back to the wholesaling community. This section will discuss the importance of sharing your knowledge and experiences with others. Mentor aspiring wholesalers, contribute to real estate forums and publications, and participate in speaking engagements and industry events. By giving back, you will not only contribute to the growth of others but also continue learning and refining your skills.

12.10 Celebrate Milestones and Achievements:

Finally, remember to celebrate your milestones and achievements along the way. This section will discuss the importance of acknowledging your progress and appreciating your hard work and dedication. Celebrate your closed deals, reached goals, and personal growth. Reward yourself for your accomplishments and use these moments as motivation to continue striving for even greater success.

Conclusion:

As you conclude your journey with "Driving for Dollars: A Ride-Share Driver's Untold Story," you now have a comprehensive roadmap to guide your ongoing success as a real estate wholesaler. By revisiting your goals, refining your strategies, continuously learning and growing, embracing technology, expanding your network, staying informed, and giving back, you will lay a solid foundation for sustainable and prosperous wholesaling endeavors.

Remember that success is a continuous journey, and each step you take brings new opportunities for growth and achievement. Stay dedicated, adaptable, and focused on your vision. Embrace the challenges, celebrate the victories, and enjoy the fulfilling and rewarding experience of being a real estate wholesaler.

Chapter 13

Overcoming Challenges and Building Resilience

This chapter will explore the inevitable challenges you may face as a real estate wholesaler and provide strategies for overcoming obstacles and building resilience. With the right mindset and tools, you can navigate through challenges and emerge more substantial on your journey to success.

13.1 Embracing the Nature of Challenges:

Challenges are an inherent part of any business, including wholesaling. This section will discuss the importance of embracing challenges as opportunities for growth. Rather than viewing challenges as setbacks, embrace them as learning experiences that push you to develop new skills, refine your strategies, and build resilience. Reframing your perspective can turn challenges into stepping stones for success.

13.2 Identifying Common Challenges in Wholesaling:

Understanding the common challenges in wholesaling is essential for proactively addressing them. In this section, we will explore some of the common challenges wholesalers may face, such as:

1. Market fluctuations and competition

2. Financing constraints and funding limitations

3. Dealing with difficult sellers and cash buyers

4. Managing tight timelines and deadlines

5. Navigating legal and regulatory complexities

6. Overcoming self-doubt and maintaining motivation

By recognizing these challenges, you can prepare to face them head-on and develop strategies to overcome them.

13.3 Developing Problem-Solving Skills:

Developing strong problem-solving skills is crucial for overcoming challenges in wholesaling. In this section, we will discuss strategies for enhancing your problem-solving abilities. We will explore techniques such as analyzing problems from different perspectives, brainstorming creative solutions, seeking input from mentors or peers, and leveraging your network for support. By becoming a skilled problem solver, you can confidently navigate obstacles and find innovative solutions.

13.4 Building Resilience and Mental Toughness:

Building resilience and mental toughness is essential for maintaining motivation and overcoming setbacks. This section will discuss strategies for cultivating resilience in the face of challenges. We will explore techniques for managing stress, practicing self-care, fostering a positive mindset, and developing a support system. Building resilience allows you to bounce back from setbacks, stay focused on your goals, and persevere through difficult times.

13.5 Seeking Support and Collaboration:

Seeking support and collaboration is vital during challenging times. This section will discuss the importance of building a support network. This can include joining real estate investing groups, attending networking events, seeking mentorship, and connecting with other wholesalers. By surrounding yourself with like-minded individuals, you can gain valuable insights, share experiences, and find encouragement when facing challenges.

13.6 Adapting to Changing Market Conditions:

Adapting to changing market conditions is critical for long-term success in wholesaling. This section will discuss strategies for staying agile and flexible in response to market fluctuations. We will explore techniques like monitoring market trends, analyzing data, adjusting your strategies, and exploring new opportunities. By embracing change and adapting your approach, you can position yourself for continued success even in dynamic market environments.

13.7 Learning from Failure:

Failure is an opportunity for growth and learning. This section will discuss the importance of embracing failure as a valuable teacher. We will explore techniques for analyzing and learning from past mistakes, adjusting your strategies based on lessons learned, and maintaining a growth mindset. By viewing failure as a stepping stone to success, you can become more resilient and make better-informed decisions in the future.

13.8 Maintaining a Positive Mindset:

Maintaining a positive mindset is vital to overcoming challenges and staying motivated. In this section, we will discuss strategies for cultivating a positive outlook. This includes practicing gratitude, visualization, positive affirmations, and self-reflection. By maintaining a positive mindset, you can navigate challenges with optimism, find solutions more efficiently, and maintain the motivation to achieve your goals.

As you conclude this chapter, remember that the wholesaling journey has inherent challenges. You can overcome obstacles and thrive in the real estate industry by embracing challenges, developing problem-solving skills, building resilience, seeking support, adapting to market conditions, learning from failure, and maintaining a positive mindset.

Every challenge you encounter is an opportunity for growth and refinement. Stay persistent, focus on your goals, and remember why you started this journey. With determination, perseverance, and the strategies provided in this chapter, you have the tools to overcome any challenge that comes your way and emerge more substantial on your path to success as a real estate wholesaler.

Chapter 14:

The Legacy of a Wholesaling Entrepreneur

This chapter will explore leaving a lasting legacy as a wholesaling entrepreneur. As you near the end of your journey, it's essential to reflect on the impact you can make and the legacy you can leave behind in the real estate industry.

14.1 Defining Your Legacy:

Defining your legacy is a deeply personal and meaningful endeavor. This section will discuss the importance of reflecting on your values, vision, and purpose. Consider the impact you want to make in the real estate industry and the lives of others. Your legacy can encompass various aspects, such as inspiring and mentoring future wholesalers, contributing to the community, or even reshaping the industry through innovation and ethical business practices.

14.2 Sharing Knowledge and Mentoring Others:

Sharing your knowledge and mentoring others is a powerful way to leave a lasting impact. In this section, we will discuss the importance of paying it forward. Consider becoming a mentor to aspiring wholesalers, sharing your experiences and insights and helping them navigate their journeys. By empowering and supporting others, you contribute to the growth and success of the wholesaling community.

14.3 Giving Back to the Community:

Giving back to the community is an opportunity to leave a positive mark beyond real estate. In this section, we will explore strategies for philanthropy and community involvement. Consider supporting local initiatives, charitable causes, and organizations that align with your values. By making a difference in the lives of others, you create a legacy of compassion and social responsibility.

14.4 Fostering Ethical Business Practices:

Ethical business practices form the foundation of a lasting legacy. This section will discuss the importance of conducting your wholesaling business with integrity, honesty, and transparency. Consider the impact of your actions on sellers, cash buyers, and the industry's overall reputation. You establish a legacy of professionalism and credibility by upholding ethical standards and fostering trust.

14.5 Innovating and Pushing Boundaries:

Innovation and pushing boundaries can redefine the wholesaling landscape and leave a legacy of progress. This section will explore the importance of embracing change and seeking new ways to improve the industry. Consider leveraging technology, embracing emerging trends, and challenging conventional practices. You create a legacy of advancement and forward-thinking by being a catalyst for innovation.

14.6 Inspiring Future Wholesalers:

Inspiring future wholesalers is a powerful way to leave a legacy of impact. In this section, we will discuss strategies for inspiring and motivating others. Share your success story, speak at industry events, and engage with aspiring wholesalers through online platforms or local meetups. By demonstrating what's possible, you ignite the entrepreneurial spirit in others and leave a legacy of inspiration.

14.7 Documenting and Preserving Your Journey:

Documenting and preserving your journey is a valuable way to ensure that your legacy lives on. This section will discuss recording your experiences, insights, and lessons learned. Consider writing a book, blogging, or sharing your story through various mediums. By preserving your wisdom and experiences, you contribute to the collective knowledge of the wholesaling community and leave a lasting impact.

14.8 Reflecting on Your Journey and Celebrating Achievements:

As you conclude your journey, take the time to reflect on how far you've come and celebrate your achievements. This section will discuss the importance of self-reflection and acknowledging your growth and successes. Consider the challenges you've overcome, the lives you've impacted, and the milestones you've reached. Recognizing and celebrating your achievements reinforces your legacy and inspires others to follow in your footsteps.

Remember that your impact on others and the industry shapes your legacy as a wholesaling entrepreneur. Define your legacy, share your knowledge, give back to the community, foster ethical practices, embrace innovation, inspire others, document your journey, and celebrate your achievements.

Your legacy will extend beyond the deals you close and your profits. It will be measured by the lives you touch, the positive changes you bring, and the inspiration you provide to those who follow in your footsteps. Embrace the opportunity to leave a lasting legacy and continue making a difference in the real estate world.

Chapter 15:

The Journey Continues: A Wholesaling Entrepreneur's Growth

This chapter will explore a wholesaling entrepreneur's ongoing growth and development. As you near the end of this book, it's essential to recognize that the journey doesn't end here. Instead, it marks the beginning of a new phase where you continue to evolve, expand, and achieve tremendous success in your wholesaling business.

15.1 Embracing a Growth Mindset:

Embracing a growth mindset is fundamental to your growth as a wholesaling entrepreneur. This section will discuss the power of believing in your ability to learn, improve, and adapt. Cultivate a mindset that embraces challenges, sees failures as opportunities for growth, and seeks continuous learning. Adopting a growth mindset will give you confidence and resilience to new challenges.

15.2 Continuous Learning and Professional Development:

Continuous learning and professional development are essential components of your growth journey. This section will explore strategies for expanding your knowledge and skills. Attend industry conferences, enroll in courses or certifications, read books and industry publications, and seek mentorship from experienced professionals. By committing to lifelong learning, you will stay ahead of industry trends, refine your expertise, and make informed decisions.

15.3 Evaluating and Refining Your Business Strategies:

Evaluating and refining your business strategies is crucial for sustained growth. This section will discuss the importance of regularly assessing your business operations, lead-generation methods, marketing strategies, and deal analysis techniques. Continuously evaluate the effectiveness of your approaches, identify areas for improvement, and adapt your strategies to align with market dynamics. Refining your business strategies will optimize efficiency, profitability, and long-term success.

15.4 Scaling and Expanding Your Wholesaling Business:

Scaling and expanding your wholesaling business is a natural progression on your growth journey. This section will explore strategies for scaling your operations and expanding into new markets or niches. Consider hiring additional team members, delegating tasks, implementing systems and processes, and leveraging technology to streamline operations. By scaling your business, you can handle a higher volume of transactions and reach new levels of success.

15.5 Building and Nurturing Relationships:

Building and nurturing relationships is a cornerstone of your growth as a wholesaling entrepreneur. This section will discuss the importance of networking, collaborating with industry professionals, and cultivating strong relationships with sellers, cash buyers, and other stakeholders. Attend real estate events, join industry associations, and engage in online communities to expand your network. You can access valuable opportunities, referrals, and support by nurturing relationships.

15.6 Leveraging Technology and Innovation:

Leveraging technology and innovation is critical to staying competitive in the evolving real estate industry. This section will explore technological advancements and innovative tools to enhance your wholesaling business. Embrace customer relationship management (CRM) software, automation tools, data analytics platforms, and other technological solutions to streamline operations, improve efficiency, and gain a competitive edge. By leveraging technology, you can unlock new growth opportunities and stay at the forefront of the industry.

15.7 Balancing Work and Personal Life:

Balancing work and personal life is vital for your well-being and continued growth. This section will discuss strategies for maintaining a healthy work-life balance. Set boundaries, prioritize self-care, and allocate time for family, hobbies, and personal growth. Remember that your personal fulfillment and happiness are critical to your success as an entrepreneur. You will have the energy and motivation to sustain your growth journey by achieving balance.

15.8 Giving Back and Leaving a Lasting Impact:

As your journey continues, consider the legacy you want to leave behind. In this section, we will explore ways to give back and make a positive impact on others. Mentor aspiring wholesalers, contribute to industry knowledge through writing or speaking engagements, and engage in philanthropic endeavors. By giving back, you create a legacy of inspiration and contribute to the growth and advancement of the wholesaling community.

It is just the beginning of a new chapter filled with growth, challenges, and opportunities. Embrace a growth mindset, commit to continuous learning, evaluate and refine your strategies, scale your business, nurture relationships, leverage technology, maintain balance, and leave a lasting impact.

As you embark on this next phase, remember that growth is a lifelong process. Embrace the journey with enthusiasm, persistence, and a hunger for knowledge and improvement. Your potential as a wholesaling entrepreneur is limitless, and by following the strategies outlined in this chapter, you can

Chapter 16:

The Future of Wholesaling: Trends and Innovations

This chapter will explore the future of wholesaling and the trends and innovations shaping the industry. As a forward-thinking wholesaling entrepreneur, it's crucial to stay informed about emerging technologies, market dynamics, and shifts in consumer behavior. By understanding these trends, you can position yourself for continued success and thrive in the ever-evolving world of real estate wholesaling.

16.1 Technological Advancements:

Technological advancements are revolutionizing the way wholesaling is conducted. This section will discuss the impact of artificial intelligence, automation, and big data analytics technologies. These advancements can streamline lead generation, improve deal analysis, enhance marketing strategies, and provide valuable insights into market trends and buyer preferences. By leveraging technology, you can gain a competitive edge and maximize efficiency in your wholesaling business.

16.2 Online Platforms and Marketplaces:

Online platforms and marketplaces are reshaping the wholesaling landscape. In this section, we will explore the rise of digital platforms that connect wholesalers with cash buyers and sellers. These platforms provide increased accessibility, transparency, and efficiency in deal transactions. By embracing online platforms, you can expand your reach, access a larger pool of buyers and sellers, and simplify connecting with potential partners.

16.3 Virtual Wholesaling:

Virtual wholesaling is becoming increasingly popular, enabling wholesalers to conduct business remotely. In this section, we will discuss the benefits and challenges of virtual wholesaling. You can use virtual tools such as video conferencing, virtual property tours, and electronic document signing to operate in multiple markets without being physically present. By embracing virtual wholesaling, you can broaden your opportunities and overcome geographical limitations.

16.4 Sustainable and Green Wholesaling:

Sustainability and environmental consciousness are emerging as essential considerations in the real estate industry. This section will discuss the growing trend of sustainable and green wholesaling. Buyers and sellers are increasingly interested in energy-efficient properties, eco-friendly materials, and sustainable practices. By incorporating sustainability into your wholesaling strategies, you can attract environmentally conscious buyers and align with the evolving market demands.

16.5 Social Media and Digital Marketing:

Social media and digital marketing continue to play a significant role in wholesaling. This section will explore the power of social media platforms, such as Facebook, Instagram, LinkedIn, and YouTube, as marketing and lead-generation channels. We will discuss strategies for creating engaging content, building an online presence, and reaching a wider audience. By leveraging social media and digital marketing, you can amplify your brand, attract motivated sellers and cash buyers, and build valuable connections.

16.6 Remote Work and Collaboration:

The rise of remote work and collaboration has reshaped how businesses operate, including wholesaling. This section will discuss the benefits and challenges of remote work and collaboration. By embracing remote work tools and collaboration platforms, you can assemble a distributed team, access talent from different locations, and facilitate seamless communication and collaboration. Embracing remote work can enhance your whole-saling business's flexibility, efficiency, and produc-tivity.

16.7 Evolving Consumer Preferences:

Consumer preferences and behavior in the real estate market are continuously evolving. This sec-tion will discuss the importance of understanding and adapting to changing consumer preferences. Buyers increasingly seek personalized experiences, convenient digital transactions, and value-added services. By staying attuned to these preferences, you can tailor your wholesaling strategies to meet the evolving needs of buyers and sellers.

16.8 Ethical and Transparent Practices:

Ethical and transparent practices are gaining prominence in the wholesaling industry. This sec-tion will explore the importance of conducting busi-ness with integrity, honesty, and transparency. Strive for fair and ethical dealings with sellers, cash buyers, and industry professionals. By fostering trust, you can build a solid reputation, attract more business, and contribute to the overall positive perception of wholesaling as a legitimate and valuable service.

16.9 Regulatory and Legal Considerations:

Regulatory and legal considerations continue to shape the wholesaling landscape. This section will discuss the importance of staying informed about local regulations, licensing requirements, and compliance obligations. Comply with laws and regulations governing wholesaling practices to protect your business and maintain credibility in the industry. Understanding and adhering to the legal framework allows you to navigate the complex regulatory landscape and ensure sustainable growth.

16.10 Embracing Change and Adaptability:

The future of wholesaling is marked by change and adaptability. This section will emphasize the importance of embracing change and being adaptable. The real estate industry is dynamic, and staying agile is crucial for long-term success. Embrace new technologies, market trends, and consumer preferences. Continuously evaluate and adjust your strategies to align with the evolving landscape. By embracing change, you position yourself as a forward-thinking wholesaling entrepreneur prepared for future growth.

As you conclude this chapter, remember that the future of wholesaling holds exciting possibilities and challenges. By staying informed about technological advancements, online platforms, virtual wholesaling, sustainable practices, social media, evolving consumer preferences, ethical practices, regulatory considerations, and embracing change, you can position yourself for continued success and growth.

Embrace the opportunities that emerging trends and innovations present. Stay adaptable, open-minded, and proactive in your approach. By continuously learning, evolving, and

Chapter 17

The Wholesaling Entrepreneur's Success Mindset

In this chapter, we will explore the success mindset that is crucial for a wholesaling entrepreneur. Developing and nurturing the right mindset is the foundation for achieving your goals, overcoming obstacles, and experiencing long-term success in the real estate industry. Let's dive into the critical elements of a success mindset and how you can cultivate it.

17.1 Clarity of Vision and Purpose:

A clear vision and purpose is essential for success as a wholesaling entrepreneur. This section will discuss the importance of defining your vision and purpose. Clarify your long-term goals, the impact you want to make, and the legacy you want to leave. By aligning your actions with your vision and purpose, you will stay focused, motivated, and driven to achieve your wholesaling goals.

17.2 Self-Belief and Confidence:

Self-belief and confidence are crucial elements of a success mindset. In this section, we will explore strategies for building self-belief and confidence. Cultivate a positive self-image, celebrate achievements, and remind yourself of your strengths and capabilities. Surround yourself with supportive individuals who believe in you and your abilities. By fostering self-belief and confidence, you will approach challenges with resilience and take bold actions to achieve success.

17.3 Resilience and Perseverance:

Resilience and perseverance are key traits that differentiate successful wholesalers. In this section, we will discuss strategies for developing resilience and perseverance. Embrace setbacks as learning opportunities, maintain a positive attitude in facing challenges, and bounce back from failures with determination. Develop coping mechanisms to manage stress and setbacks. You will overcome obstacles and stay committed to your wholesaling journey by cultivating resilience and perseverance.

17.4 Embracing a Growth Mindset:

Embracing a growth mindset is vital for continuous learning and improvement. In this section, we will explore the characteristics of a growth mindset. See challenges as opportunities for growth, view failures as stepping stones to success, and embrace the journey of learning and development. Adopt a mindset that seeks new knowledge, welcomes feedback, and embraces change. You will continuously evolve and adapt to the ever-changing real estate industry by cultivating a growth mindset.

17.5 Goal Setting and Planning:

Goal setting and planning are critical for turning your vision into reality. In this section, we will discuss effective goal-setting techniques. Set specific, measurable, attainable, relevant, and time-bound (SMART) goals. Break them into actionable steps and create a roadmap to guide your progress. Regularly review and adjust your goals as needed. You will stay focused and motivated on your wholesaling journey by setting clear goals and developing actionable plans.

17.6 Continuous Learning and Personal Development:

Continuous learning and personal development are key elements of a success mindset. This section will discuss the importance of investing in your knowledge and skills. Commit to lifelong learning through reading books, attending seminars, enrolling in courses, and seeking mentorship. Embrace personal development practices such as journaling, meditation, and self-reflection. By continuously expanding your knowledge and developing yourself, you will enhance your abilities and stay ahead in the competitive real estate industry.

17.7 Embracing Accountability:

Embracing accountability is crucial for achieving your wholesaling goals. This section will discuss the importance of owning your actions and outcomes. Hold yourself accountable for your commitments, deadlines, and results. Surround yourself with an accountability partner or join a mastermind group to foster a sense of responsibility. You will maintain discipline, productivity, and progress toward your wholesaling goals by embracing accountability.

17.8 Building Relationships and Collaboration:

Building relationships and fostering collaboration is a vital aspect of a success mindset. This section will explore the power of networking and collaboration in the real estate industry. Seek opportunities to connect with industry professionals, investors, and potential partners—nurture relationships based on trust, integrity, and mutual support. Collaborate on deals and share knowledge and resources. Building strong relationships and fostering collaboration will create a supportive network that can fuel your wholesaling success.

17.9 Positive Mindset and Gratitude:

Maintaining a positive mindset and practicing gratitude can significantly impact your wholesaling journey. In this section, we will discuss the importance of positivity and gratitude. Cultivate an optimistic outlook, focus on solutions rather than problems, and practice gratitude for the opportunities and successes you experience. Adopting a positive mindset and expressing gratitude will attract positivity, resilience, and abundance into your wholesaling business.

As a wholesaling entrepreneur, cultivating a success mindset is essential for achieving your goals, overcoming challenges, and experiencing long-term success in the real estate industry. Embrace clarity of vision and purpose, develop self-belief and confidence, cultivate resilience and perseverance, adopt a growth mindset, set goals and plan strategically, prioritize continuous learning and personal development, embrace accountability, build relationships and collaboration, and maintain a positive mindset and gratitude.

Remember that your mindset is a powerful force that can propel you forward or hold you back. Choose a success mindset that empowers you, supports your wholesaling journey, and helps you achieve your desired outcomes. Your mindset will shape your actions, decisions, and

Chapter 18:

The Realty Titan's Wholesaling Toolbox

Introduction:

This chapter will explore the essential tools and resources that will empower you as a wholesaling entrepreneur. Building a well-equipped toolbox is crucial for streamlining your operations, maximizing efficiency, and achieving success in the competitive real estate market. Let's dive into the essential tools and resources you need to thrive in wholesaling.

18.1 Customer Relationship Management (CRM) Software:

Customer Relationship Management (CRM) software is valuable for managing leads, contacts, and deals. This section will discuss the benefits of using a CRM system. Capture and organize leads, track communications, schedule follow-ups, and manage your pipeline efficiently. CRM software lets you stay organized, nurture relationships, and effectively close deals.

18.2 Lead-Generation Tools:

Lead generation is the lifeblood of your wholesaling business. In this section, we will explore various lead-generation tools and strategies. Utilize online platforms like Zillow, Realtor.com, and Redfin to identify potential leads. Consider using lead-generation software or services that provide targeted lists, skip-tracing services, and contact information for distressed property owners. You can access a consistent stream of motivated sellers by leveraging lead-generation tools to fuel your wholesaling deals.

18.3 Deal Analysis Software:

Accurate deal analysis is critical for making informed investment decisions. In this section, we will discuss deal analysis software. Use tools like RehabEstimatorPro, FlipAnalyzer, DealMachine, or BiggerPockets' Calculators to evaluate potential deals, estimate repair costs, analyze ARV (After Repair Value), and calculate profits. Deal analysis software helps you assess the viability of a deal and make data-driven decisions.

18.4 Online Listing and Marketing Platforms:

Online listing and marketing platforms enable you to showcase your properties and attract potential cash buyers. This section will explore popular platforms like MLS, Zillow, Trulia, and Craigslist. Create compelling property listings with detailed descriptions, high-quality photos, and virtual tours. Leverage social media platforms to promote your listings and engage with potential buyers. You can increase visibility, attract qualified cash buyers, and expedite sales by utilizing online listing and marketing platforms.

18.5 Document Management and Electronic Signature Tools:

Efficient document management and electronic signature tools are essential for seamless deal transactions. This section will discuss platforms like DocuSign, HelloSign, or Adobe Sign. Digitize your paperwork, create templates for standard documents, and enable electronic signatures to expedite the contract signing process. Document management and electronic signature tools save time, reduce paperwork, and enhance the efficiency of your wholesaling business.

18.6 Networking and Collaboration Platforms:

Networking and collaboration are key to expanding your wholesaling network and accessing valuable opportunities. This section will explore platforms like BiggerPockets, LinkedIn, and real estate investing groups. Join online forums, participate in discussions, and connect with like-minded wholesalers, investors, and industry professionals. Collaboration platforms like Slack or Trello can facilitate seamless communication and project management. You can build a strong network, gain insights, and foster partnerships by leveraging networking and collaboration platforms.

18.7 Real Estate Investing Education and Mentorship:

Continuous learning and mentorship are invaluable resources for your wholesaling journey. This section will discuss the importance of investing in real estate education and seeking mentorship. Attend workshops, seminars, and webinars to enhance your knowledge and skills. Consider joining mentorship programs or seeking guidance from experienced wholesalers who can provide valuable insights and guidance. Real estate investing education and mentorship accelerate your learning curve, expand your perspectives, and shorten your path to success.

18.8 Local Real Estate Associations and Meetups:

Local real estate associations and meetups offer opportunities for networking, learning, and accessing local market insights. This section will discuss the benefits of joining local real estate associations and attending meetups. Engage with industry professionals, exchange knowledge and experiences, and stay informed about local market trends. Participating in local real estate associations and meetups can build relationships, gain credibility, and stay connected with the local real estate community.

18.9 Professional Service Providers:

Establishing relationships with reliable, professional service providers is crucial for a smooth wholesaling operation. This section will explore essential professionals like real estate attorneys, title companies, contractors, and property inspectors. Collaborate with professionals specializing in real estate transactions, property repairs, and due diligence. Establishing a network of trusted professionals ensures your deals proceed smoothly and minimizes potential risks.

18.10 Books, Podcasts, and Industry Publications:

Books, podcasts, and industry publications provide wholesalers with a wealth of knowledge and inspiration. This section will emphasize the importance of continuous learning through reading books, listening to podcasts, and staying updated with industry publications. Explore titles like "The Book on Investing in Real Estate with No (and Low) Money Down" by Brandon Turner, or listen to real estate podcasts like "The Real Estate Titans" or "Bigger-Pockets Real Estate Podcast." By immersing yourself in industry resources, you can gain insights from seasoned experts, learn from their experiences, and refine your wholesaling strategies.

Building a well-equipped wholesaling toolbox sets you up for success in the real estate industry. Utilize customer relationship management (CRM) software, lead-generation tools, deal analysis software, online listing, and marketing platforms, document management and electronic signature tools, networking and collaboration platforms, real estate investing education and mentorship, local real estate associations and meetups, professional service providers, and industry resources to streamline your operations, maximize efficiency, and achieve wholesaling success.

Remember to continuously evaluate and update your toolbox as new technologies and resources emerge in the industry. Adapt to market trends and leverage the tools and resources that align with your business goals and preferences. Equipping yourself with the right tools allows you to position yourself for success and growth as a wholesaling entrepreneur.

Best of luck as you utilize your wholesaling toolbox to navigate the dynamic real estate market and

Conclusion:

Congratulations on completing "Driving for Dollars: A Ride-Share Driver's Untold Story - The Realty Titan's Guide to Wholesaling Real Estate without Using Your Own Money." Throughout this book, we have embarked on a transformative journey that has empowered you with the knowledge, strategies, and mindset necessary to succeed as a wholesaling entrepreneur.

As a ride-share driver turned real estate wholesaler, you have discovered the immense potential within your reach. By leveraging your time on the road and adopting a keen eye for distressed properties, you can uncover hidden gems and turn them into profitable deals. Through the practice of "driving for dollars," you have learned to spot opportunities where others see only challenges.

In each chapter, we delved into critical aspects of wholesaling, including understanding the market, finding motivated sellers, analyzing deals, negotiating contracts, and building a strong buyer's list. We explored the power of networking, marketing, and leveraging technology to streamline your operations and maximize your profits. Additionally, we discussed the importance of maintaining a success mindset, embracing continuous learning, and leaving a lasting legacy in the industry.

Remember that wholesaling is not without its challenges. It requires dedication, perseverance, and adapting to changing market conditions. As you embark on your wholesaling journey, keep in mind the following key takeaways:

1. Knowledge is power: Continuously educate yourself about the real estate industry, market trends, and investment strategies. Stay informed through books, podcasts, industry publications, and professional networking.

2. Building relationships is essential: Cultivate a strong network of industry contacts, including motivated sellers, cash buyers, investors, and professionals. Collaborate with others, share knowledge, and create win-win partnerships.

3. Embrace technology and innovation: Leverage the power of technology, CRM software, lead-generation tools, online marketing platforms, and other tools to streamline your operations, increase efficiency, and reach a broader audience.

4. Maintain integrity and ethical practices: Uphold ethical standards in all your dealings. Transparency, honesty, and integrity build trust with sellers, buyers, and industry professionals, ensuring your long-term success.

5. Develop a success mindset: Cultivate self-belief, resilience, perseverance, and a growth mindset. Set clear goals, stay focused, and adapt to challenges.

Remember, this journey is just the beginning. As you implement the strategies outlined in this book, you will gain valuable experience, refine your skills, and achieve success beyond your wildest dreams. Embrace each step of your journey, learn from your experiences, and keep pushing forward.

Always remember that success is not solely measured by monetary gains but also by the positive impact you make in the lives of others. Share your knowledge, mentor aspiring wholesalers, give back to your community, and leave a lasting legacy as a Realty Titan.

Now it's time to embark on your path as a real estate wholesaler. Embrace the challenges, seize the opportunities, and never stop learning and growing. The real estate industry is ever-evolving, and as a driven and resourceful individual, you have the power to shape your own success.

Best of luck on your wholesaling journey, and may your passion, determination, and resilience guide you to new heights in the exciting world of real estate.

.

Appendix

Congratulations on completing "Driving for Dollars: A Ride-Share Driver's Untold Story - The Realty Titan's Guide to Wholesaling Real Estate without Using Your Own Money." In this appendix, you will find additional resources and tools to support you in your wholesaling journey. These resources are designed to provide further guidance, education, and assistance as you navigate the dynamic real estate market. Let's explore the valuable resources available to you:

1. Recommended Books:

Here are some highly recommended books that can enhance your knowledge and skills in real estate wholesaling:

- "The Book on Investing in Real Estate with No (and Low) Money Down" by Brandon Turner

- "The Wholesaling Blueprint: The Complete Guide to Real Estate Wholesaling" by Luke Weber

- "The Millionaire Real Estate Investor" by Gary Keller

- "The Art of Wholesaling Properties: How to Buy and Sell Real Estate without Cash or Credit" by Aram Shah and Alex Virelles

2. Online Platforms and Communities:

Engaging with online platforms and communities can provide valuable insights, networking opportunities, and support. Consider joining the following platforms and communities:

- BiggerPockets (www.biggerpockets.com): An online community of real estate investors and professionals offering forums, articles, podcasts, and educational resources.

- Real Estate Investing Forums (www.realestateforums.net): A platform for real estate investors to discuss various topics, ask questions, and share insights.

- LinkedIn Groups: Join relevant LinkedIn groups focused on real estate investing, wholesaling, and networking.

3. Wholesaling Courses and Programs:

Taking specialized courses or programs can provide in-depth knowledge and step-by-step guidance on wholesaling. Consider enrolling in the following programs:

- Wholesaling Inc. (www.wholesalinginc.com): Offers comprehensive wholesaling education, coaching, and resources.

- FortuneBuilders (www.fortunebuilders.com): Provides real estate investing education, including wholesaling, through workshops, courses, and mentorship programs.

4. Real Estate Investing Podcasts:

Podcasts are an excellent way to learn from experienced professionals and stay updated on industry trends. Consider listening to the following real estate investing podcasts:

- BiggerPockets Real Estate Podcast

- The Real Estate Titans Podcast

- The Wholesaling Inc. Podcast

5. Real Estate Investing Events and Conferences:

Attending industry events and conferences can expand your network, provide educational opportunities, and expose you to new ideas and strategies. Keep an eye out for real estate investing events and conferences in your local area, or consider attending national events such as:

- The Real Estate Success Summit

- National Real Estate Investor's Conference (NREI Expo)

- Real Estate Wholesaling Summit

6. Legal and Compliance Resources:

Staying informed about legal and compliance requirements in the real estate industry is essential. Consult with legal professionals and refer to resources such as:

- Local real estate laws and regulations: Familiarize yourself with the laws and regulations specific to your area.

- State and national real estate associations: Access resources and information related to legal and compliance matters through these associations.

Remember to conduct due diligence and consult professionals when making legal or financial decisions.

Conclusion:

This appendix provides a starting point for accessing additional resources and tools to support your wholesaling journey. The recommended books, online platforms, communities, courses, podcasts, events, and legal resources mentioned here will help you expand your knowledge, network with like-minded individuals, and stay updated with industry trends and compliance requirements.

As a Realty Titan, your commitment to continuous learning, networking, and personal development will set you apart in the competitive real estate market. Stay motivated, remain adaptable, and embrace new opportunities as they arise. With determination and the right resources, you have the potential to achieve remarkable success as a wholesaling entrepreneur.

Best of luck as you utilize these resources to enhance your wholesaling skills further and propel your real estate business to new heights.

Note: The information in this book and appendix is for educational purposes only. It is not intended as financial, legal, or professional advice. Readers should consult with appropriate professionals before making any investment or business decisions.